J 599.658 Vog

Vogel, J.
Caribou.

PRICE: $12.95 (3582/04   )

D1384597

Date Due

NOV 0 9 2006			
AUG 1 4 2008			
SEP 0 2 2008			

BRODART, INC.   Cat. No. 23 233   Printed in U.S.A.

TOWN OF CALEDON PUBLIC LIBRARY

Our WILD™
WORLD
SERIES

Caribou

NorthWord Press
Chanhassen, Minnesota

TOWN OF CALEDON PUBLIC LIBRARY

DEDICATION
For Paula and Gail, friends and partners in writing and other adventures.
Special thanks to caribou biologist Anne Gunn, Ph.D., for sharing her knowledge and expertise.

© NorthWord Press, 2002

Photography © 2002: Tim Christie/www.timchristie.com: cover; Craig Brandt: pp. 4, 19, 25, 41, 44; Tom Vezo: pp. 5, 26-27; Tom Walker: pp. 6, 17, 22-23, 32-33, 34, 35; Art Wolfe: pp. 8-9; Jim Brandenburg/Minden Pictures: p. 11; Wayne Lynch: pp. 12-13; Vic Van Ballenberghe: p. 14; Mark Raycroft: pp. 16, 38-39; Michio Hoshino/Minden Pictures: pp. 20, 29; Don Jones: p. 40; Gene & Jason Stone/Leeson Photography pp. 42-43; Robin Brandt: back cover.

Illustrations by John F. McGee
Designed by Russell S. Kuepper
Edited by Barbara K. Harold

NorthWord Press
18705 Lake Drive East
Chanhassen, MN 55317
1-800-328-3895
www.northwordpress.com

All rights reserved. No part of this work covered by the copyrights hereon may be reproduced or used in any form or by any means—graphic, electronic or mechanical, including photocopying, recording, taping of information on storage and retrieval systems—without the prior written permission of the publisher.

The copyright on each photograph in this book belongs to the photographer, and no reproductions of the photographic images contained herein may be made without the express permission of the photographer.

Library of Congress Cataloging-in-Publication Data

Vogel, Julia.
    Caribou / Julia Vogel ; illustrations by John F. McGee.
        p. cm. -- (Our wild world series)
    Summary: Discusses the physical characteristics, habitat, behavior, and life cycle of caribou, members of the deer family.
    ISBN 1-55971-813-7 (hc.) -- ISBN 1-55971-812-9 (softcover)
    1. Caribou--Juvenile literature. [1. Caribou.] I. McGee, John F., ill. II. Title. III. Series.

QL737.U55 V64 2002
599.65'8--dc21   2001057932

Printed in Singapore

10 9 8 7 6 5 4 3 2 1

Our **WILD**™ **WORLD** SERIES

Caribou

Julia Vogel
Illustrations by John F. McGee

NORTHWORD PRESS
Chanhassen, Minnesota

CARIBOU ARE ALWAYS on the move. Every spring, large groups, or herds, march north to spend the summer near the Arctic Ocean. Every fall, they journey south again for the winter. World-champion walkers, caribou have followed the same trails through northern wilderness for thousands of years. This seasonal movement is called migration. For caribou, migration may be hundreds of miles long!

These ancient wanderers make their home in one of the harshest places on Earth. They must withstand the Arctic's strong winds, deep snow, and frigid temperatures. How do caribou survive in this frozen land?

Caribou antlers come in all sizes and shapes. This male's unique antlers can be used to easily identify him.

A young caribou is called a calf. It stays near its mother for protection and for food.

Like caribou this reindeer has excellent senses. It can hear and see especially well. And its sense of smell is much better than a human's.

Caribou belong to a group of large mammals, the deer family. Moose, whitetail deer, and elk are also members of this family. All kinds of deer share important features, or traits, that help them survive. Long necks help them see far to spot danger, and slim legs provide power for quick escapes. Hooves, or hard coverings on their feet, grip the ground wherever they walk. And members of the deer family are the only animals that grow bony antlers on their heads, which they use to fight off predators (PRED-uh-torz), or animals that kill them for food.

Moose and elk also live in cold climates, but caribou live farther north than any of their close relatives. Caribou are stockier and have shorter legs than many other family members. These are two traits that help them stay warm.

During the last Ice Age, millions of caribou roamed North America's snow fields with mammoths, mastodons, and other creatures that have become extinct, or died out. Caribou fossils have been found as far south as Tennessee and Alabama. The areas where caribou live and feed are called home ranges. As the Earth warmed, the herds' living space became smaller. Today, nearly all of North America's caribou live in Alaska and Canada.

Caribou
FUNFACT:

Caribou and reindeer belong to the same species, and have the same scientific name, *Rangifer tarandus*. There are about 3 million wild caribou in the world, plus about 2 million wild and domesticated reindeer.

Unlike caribou, reindeer males are often known as stags and females are called does.

In Europe and Asia, caribou are known by another name, reindeer. Wild reindeer look and act very much like North American caribou, although reindeer are usually a bit smaller than caribou.

Many reindeer were domesticated, or tamed, about 5,000 years ago by native people in Asia's Altai Mountains. The tribes began following the herds, defending them from wolves, and using them for milk, meat, and hides. Some reindeer have been trained to pull sleds and carry riders. A century ago, tame reindeer were brought to Alaska to be herded by Eskimos. Today, natives in Scandinavia and Russia keep large reindeer herds to make a living in their icy homelands.

Woodland Caribou

Peary Caribou

Barren-ground Caribou

Peary caribou usually live in small herds. During summer, they feast on willow, herbs, and grasses. During winter, they search for whatever is available.

North America's caribou are separated into three main types. The smallest ones, Peary caribou, live the closest to the North Pole. Their home is on a few windswept islands in Canada's High Arctic. Every winter, they face extreme cold and darkness when the sun disappears from view for many weeks.

Their silky, white coat acts as camouflage (KAM-uh-flaj) to help them blend into their snow-white habitat, or surroundings. When spring returns, Peary caribou travel to find more food and safe places to give birth on the northern parts of their islands. They may even cross frozen ice to reach other shores. Recent bad weather has made their lives harder than ever, and only about 2,000 to 3,000 Peary caribou still exist on their rocky island homes.

Woodland caribou are found farther south than Peary caribou. These caribou live in the taiga (tie-GUH), a wide area of evergreen forests that is snow-covered in winter and boggy in summer. In North America, woodland caribou once roamed the northern United States from Maine to Washington. Hunting and clearing forests for farms have caused their populations to shrink and even vanish in some areas. Now almost all woodland caribou live in Canada's taiga, from Newfoundland to British Columbia.

Woodland caribou are the largest type, with extra-long legs for plowing through deep forest snow. Woodland caribou usually do not migrate long distances between summer and winter homes. But they are constantly going somewhere, searching for food or safe places to give birth or escaping from wolves, bears, and other predators.

Scientists are not sure why caribou have a patch of long hair, called a mane, around their necks. It may help the males look bigger and stronger to the females.

Caribou are diurnal (di-YER-nul) animals. That means they are mostly active during the day, when they move around and feed.

Wandering in small, scattered groups of two to six animals, woodland caribou avoid roads, houses, and even scientists trying to study them. Logging and road-building can chase them out of a forest and keep them away for decades. The woodland caribou's secretive ways have earned them the nickname, "gray ghosts of the forest."

In the winter, the taiga's trees also shelter another type of caribou, barren-ground caribou. But every spring, these caribou migrate north to the wide-open, treeless tundra (TUN-druh). Trees cannot grow on the tundra because of its extreme cold, strong winds, and ground that never thaws completely. The summer sun can melt only the top layer of earth, creating a marshy plain, green with grasses and other small plants. Canadians call the tundra "the barrens" because it looks like a frozen desert in winter, and that's probably where barren-ground caribou got their name. But in summer, the tundra is home to many creatures, including great numbers of birds and insects.

Caribou
FUNFACT:

Three herds have more than 500,000 animals: Western Arctic caribou herd of Alaska, George River caribou herd of Canada, and Taimyr Peninsula reindeer herd of Russia. The only wild caribou in the lower 48 states are about three dozen that live part of the year in the Selkirk Mountains of Idaho and Washington.

A male's antlers are often known as his rack.
The tips of the antlers are called points.

Living from Alaska to the Hudson Bay, barren-ground caribou are by far the most common type of caribou. They live in herds of a few thousand to over 500,000 animals. They are usually lighter-colored and smaller than woodland caribou, although sizes vary widely depending on where the animals live.

Adults stand about 3 to 5 feet (0.9 to 1.5 meters) tall at the shoulder. Females, or cows, weigh between 130 and 210 pounds (60 and 95 kilograms). Males, or bulls, may weigh as much as 175 to 400 pounds (80 to 180 kilograms).

Barren-ground males carry the widest and longest antlers of any caribou. One record pair was 46 inches (117 centimeters) wide and 51 inches (130 centimeters) long.

When caribou like this barren-ground herd graze, they move quickly.

But the barren-ground caribou's most spectacular feature is their seasonal migration. Depending on the herd, they may travel up to 600 miles (965 kilometers) between their summer and winter ranges—the longest migration of any land animal.

Wherever barren-ground caribou travel, native people have come to depend on them. Some tribes learned to follow the herds, while others built their villages along traditional migration paths. For thousands of years, caribou hides have been made into boots, robes, leggings, and tents. Knives, scrapers, spear points, and sewing needles have been shaped from bones and antlers. Many northern communities still rely on barren-ground caribou meat to help them survive the Arctic winter.

Every caribou needs a thick fur coat for protection from wind and cold. Hair covers them from their ears to their feet. In fact, caribou and moose are the only deer family members with fur all over their muzzles, or snouts.

Two kinds of hair insulate caribou in winter. A fine, curly underfur lies close to the body, warming it like a wool sweater. Longer, stiff guard hairs stand out to shed snow and block the wind. The guard hairs are hollow, and air trapped inside them makes an extra shield against the cold. These air-filled hairs also work like a life jacket, helping caribou float when they swim across lakes and rivers.

In cold weather, lots of body heat could escape through a caribou's long legs. But a network of arteries and veins cools caribou blood before it enters the legs, then warms it again as it returns to the body. A caribou's normal body temperature is about 102 degrees Fahrenheit (39 degrees Celsius), yet its legs stay around 46 degrees Fahrenheit (8 degrees Celsius). This system keeps needed heat from escaping when the wind whips around the caribou's legs.

All mammals with hooves on their feet are called ungulates (UN-gyoo-lutz). Caribou are even-toed ungulates, as are cows, pigs, and other deer. Each caribou foot has four toes: two big toes, and two smaller toes, called dew claws. Ungulates with an odd number of toes include horses, which have one toe on each foot, and rhinoceroses, with three toes on each foot.

Caribou
FUNFACT:

Caribou click when they walk! The sound is caused by their ankle tendons slipping over bones in their feet. It doesn't hurt the animal, but a large herd trotting along the trail can be very loud.

Caribou usually have white hair around the rump and muzzle and a ring around the eyes. They also have white hair inside the ears and sometimes a white chest patch.

Caribou can find their way straight across a lake too wide to see the other side. They are good swimmers.

The edges of caribou hooves are sharp, perfect for gripping the ice or for slashing at an attacking enemy. In the water, the wide hooves act like paddles to help the animal swim. In soft snow or swampy ground, the big toes and dew claws spread out, working like snowshoes to stop the caribou from sinking. Including the dew claws, a large male's track may be almost 8 inches (20 centimeters) long and more than 5 inches (13 centimeters) wide.

Perhaps the most important job of caribou hooves is digging for food. During much of the year, almost everything caribou eat is blanketed by snow. A hungry caribou uses its hooves like scoops, making quick pawing strokes to send snow flying out of the way. It must dig snow holes, called craters, throughout the winter to avoid starvation. Micmac Indians even named the animals "xalibu" (GHAH-lee-boo), meaning snow shoveler. Many people believe the word caribou comes from that Micmac name.

How do caribou find the food that is covered by snow? They rely on their keen sense of smell. They push their long, wide snouts into the snow, searching for food smells before beginning the difficult work of digging. Just as we can smell brownies in the oven, a caribou can easily smell food under 1 foot (30 centimeters) of snow. Caribou also use their noses to recognize each other and to detect danger.

Caribou are plant-eaters, or herbivores (HERB-uh-vorz). During the short Arctic summer, their diet includes many kinds of plants. Depending on where it lives, a caribou may eat Arctic cotton-grass, willow leaves, mushrooms, and especially flower buds, which are packed with protein. An adult consumes 12 to 20 pounds (5 to 9 kilograms) per day.

Feeding grounds are not always on flat land. And bulls do not always graze alone.
A good supply of food may attract several caribou.

Winter food in the Arctic, though, is scarce. Some days, the only things to eat are a few twigs, plus some snow for moisture. Luckily, one kind of caribou food is plentiful under the snow: lichens (LIE-kenz). Lichens are found year-round in strange, colorful splotches on rocks, tree branches, and frozen soil. Caribou eat so much of one kind of lichen, it's known as "reindeer moss" or "caribou candy."

The animals' huge appetites make it hard for the lichens to survive. A herd digging into drifts and stretching into trees for food can eventually strip an area through feeding and trampling. Brittle and easily damaged by sharp hooves, lichens grow slowly, only about ¼ inch (6 millimeters) per year. It can take 50 to 100 years, or more, for a forest to recover from too much grazing. Fortunately, the animals' constant wandering helps protect the lichens.

Whether they're eating fresh grass shoots or frozen lichens, caribou nip and tear off bites using their tongue and their bottom front teeth. They don't have incisors (in-SIZE-orz), or middle teeth, in their upper jaws. Their back teeth, or molars, grind the food just enough for it to be swallowed.

The partially chewed food travels to the first chamber of the caribou's four-chamber stomach. The animal looks for a safe place to rest, such as a frozen lake where predators can't sneak up on it without being seen. Then it brings a wad of food back into its mouth for re-chewing. The wads are called cuds, and caribou, like cattle, are called cud chewers. Once the cud is thoroughly chewed, it returns to the stomach, by-passing the first chamber and moving through each of the other three chambers to complete its digestion.

Even when caribou lie down to rest while chewing their cuds, they are always aware of their surroundings and the predators that may be nearby.

If this male and female sense a danger to the herd, they call to the others.
If they run to escape, others then follow.

Even when eating or resting, caribou must stay alert to danger. Their sharp hearing helps keep them alive. The cup-shaped ears collect sounds from near and far. And by swiveling their ears, caribou can hear in almost any direction without turning their heads.

A caribou's eyes are large and can see close and far away. Positioned on the sides of the head, the eyes capture a wide field of view. Caribou don't see colors as we do. But they do see shapes clearly and can detect slight movements that a human would never notice.

At the first sign of danger, a caribou stops and sniffs the air. Then it signals the other herd members by snorting and kicking a hind leg out to the side. That's an alarm movement that all the others in a herd recognize. As the caribou leaps away, glands in its hind feet release a scent, or odor, that warns other caribou to beware of trouble. The startled caribou gallops away, then slows to a steady trot for many miles until it feels safe again.

Speed is a caribou's best defense against predators. But it may not always escape. A newborn may be grabbed in the forest by a lynx or snatched from above by a golden eagle. A mother caribou will try to defend her young by kicking or by slashing with her antlers. But she's usually no match for a grizzly bear that may be hunting to feed its own cubs.

One wild animal kills more caribou than any other: the wolf. Wolf packs follow caribou as they roam, watching and waiting. Because caribou run so fast, a single wolf rarely catches one. But a pack of wolves can work as a team. They sneak up on a caribou and ambush it, or separate a caribou from the herd, then chase it for miles to wear it down. The whole pack joins in the meal after a successful hunt.

To escape predators, caribou can run up to 50 miles per hour (80 kilometers per hour) on land. To get away, they are not afraid to run through a pond or river if necessary.

Leftovers from a wolf kill may be food for other hungry animals, such as wolverines, ravens, Arctic foxes, and even mice and voles. Biologists often call the caribou a keystone species because it is key, or important, to the survival of so many other Arctic animals.

Escaping from wolves is one reason barren-ground caribou migrate. Arctic wolves usually don't raise their young on the tundra, so most packs stay behind when the caribou herds leave the taiga in spring. Caribou also migrate to find the most nutritious food and to find the best places to live as the weather changes each season.

Longer days in springtime probably trigger the caribou's urge to travel. But how do they navigate, or find their way? Often, herds follow old trails they can clearly see on the land. But they must also climb snow-covered mountains, swim wide lakes, and wade across bogs or swamps. Have caribou memorized the routes? Are they following the wind, the stars, or Earth's magnetic clues? Researchers can now learn about caribou movements by following signals from special caribou collars, but they still haven't solved all the mysteries of caribou migration.

No matter how they navigate, we know caribou migration usually begins in April. Older, experienced cows lead the way, followed closely by other cows and last year's babies, or calves. Bulls age two and older often leave the taiga weeks later. The leading cows have the most difficult job, often needing to break through deep snow to make a good trail. The others follow single-file behind them to save energy for the long journey ahead.

Storms may slow their progress, or they may lose hours searching for a safe river crossing. Caribou in a hurry can travel up to 50 miles (80 kilometers) in a day. When they can walk no farther, the animals drop to the ground, exhausted. Yet hours later, they are up and ready to go on.

Each herd marches toward a different place on the tundra, where generations of their ancestors have been born. All caribou that share the same birthplace, or calving ground, belong to the same herd. For example, caribou born near the coast in the northeast corner of Alaska belong to the Porcupine herd. And those that return to Bluenose Lake in Canada are called the Bluenose herd.

While on the move, a caribou herd may travel in a line many miles long.
The animals often gather in groups to graze along the migration route.

At first, caribou calves are wobbly on their feet. They soon learn to keep up with their mother and the other calves in the herd.

By early June it is time for the calves to be born. Each cow separates from the herd to give birth alone. She searches for a quiet and protected place. A caribou has one calf per year, almost never twins. She licks her newborn clean, getting to know its unique smell and voice from all the other thousands of calves in her herd.

Nearly all the cows in the same herd give birth within about two weeks. This is called synchronous (SIN-kruh-nus) arrival. It helps protect the young from predators because there are too many calves to kill all at once. It also means the calves will have many playmates as they grow and learn about their habitat.

The newborns' color is reddish brown, which helps them blend into the brown tundra. But calves do not hide. They are following after their mothers within hours of their birth. In a few days the pair rejoins the herd. At seven days old, most calves can outrun a wolf.

The calves grow fast on their mother's milk, which is very rich. At birth, calves may weigh from 6 to 20 pounds (3 to 9 kilograms). Their weight doubles in about two weeks. They gain strength quickly too. Calves leap, twist, buck, chase each other, and run circles around their mothers. This is play that builds muscles and bones.

By late June, the strong summer sun turns the tundra green and calves begin nibbling on the tender plant growth. By mid-summer, most of them no longer need their mothers' milk. Caribou of all ages feast on their favorite plants. New mothers, especially, must eat as much as they can to recover from giving birth and to fatten-up for the long winter ahead.

Soon the mother takes the young caribou back to the herd, where they both will be safer.

In July, another kind of creature feasts on caribou: blood-sucking insects. Mosquitoes and biting flies hatch by the billions in the marshy tundra. At the same time, the caribou are shedding their heavy winter coat. This leaves only a thin layer of dark fur protecting their skin. The biting swarms torment and weaken the caribou. Mosquitoes can cause a caribou to lose up to 1 quart (0.95 liter) of blood each week during mosquito season.

Warm, windless days are the worst.

The fierce bites become more than the animals can stand. How they escape depends on where they live. Some climb slopes to reach cooling patches of snow. Others trot to the shore to stand in the breeze or wade into the waves. Often, groups of caribou gather together, standing tightly against one another so that each caribou has less chance of being bitten. These groups roam across the tundra, eating when they can, but moving fast to stay ahead of the insects.

The huge July gatherings make tremendous noise. The air seems filled with snorts, coughs, belches, and hoof beats. Calves bleat, or call, to their mothers, who grunt in reply. If a calf loses its mother, it stops. The mother stops too and lets the herd move on. Both trot back and forth along the trail, calling for each other, until they are reunited. But if they don't meet, the calf will probably die because another caribou cow will not adopt an orphan calf. Each cow only takes care of her own young.

True insect relief only comes with the cooler days of August. This is also the time that caribou scatter across the tundra for a final fattening-up before winter.

In early autumn, the animals begin to look different. Their new winter coats are chocolate brown, with a thick white mane on the neck and chest. Also during this time, bulls often add an extra layer of fat on the back and rump. It may be more than 3 inches (7.5 centimeters) thick. This fat will provide much needed energy during the upcoming breeding season, or rut.

But the biggest change to caribou appearance is on their heads. The adults' antlers are nearing full size, and even the calves have grown short spikes. Antlers average 20 to 51 inches (51 to 130 centimeters) long on adult males, and 9 to 20 inches (23 to 51 centimeters) long on adult females.

Caribou
FUNFACT:

Caribou recycle their own shed antlers by chewing on them to get calcium. Other creatures such as mice also nibble on the fallen antlers over the winter.

Broken branches give clues that a caribou has used a bush for antler polishing.
Even a small animal can cause lots of damage.

The horns of cattle and some other animals grow all their lives. But antlers grow in an annual cycle and are shed, or dropped, each year. Both male and female caribou grow antlers. Growth begins from permanent knobs on their skulls. At first, the developing bone is flexible and covered with soft, hairy skin called velvet.

The blood-rich velvet nourishes the antlers until they reach full size and become hard. Then the velvet starts peeling off in strips. The peeling velvet itches, so the caribou scrapes off the rest by rubbing its antlers against trees and bushes. The "polishing" reveals shiny brown antlers. Sometimes the tips are polished nearly white.

Cows have smaller antlers than bulls. Females carry antlers most of the year, shedding them after giving birth in the spring. Then new growth begins just a few weeks later. This way, caribou mothers can use their antlers to protect themselves and their calves almost year-round.

Bull antler growth follows different timing. A bull's antler buds appear in late March and continue to grow and branch out through the summer until a thick and tall beam arches high over his head on each side. The part of the antlers that grows out over the bull's snout is called the "shovel." The biggest antlers belong to older, healthy males. Like cows, bulls use antlers to fight off predators. A bull's antlers are also a sign of power that all caribou understand.

Each bull uses its strong neck muscles and sturdy legs to shove the other male as hard as he can.

The bulls are eager to show who is the strongest. They match head-to-head with other males. Which one will win? Both grunt and dig in their hooves and push. And push! They sometimes crash together, breaking off antler tips. Most sparring matches end when one male is shoved off balance and gallops away. A few end with one or both bulls suffering serious wounds.

Sparring is a sure signal that the rut has arrived. For about two weeks in October, bulls fight to win a chance to mate. They do not gather and defend groups of females. Instead, caribou bulls travel between many groups of cows and calves, looking for females ready to mate, and chasing off other males. They stop eating and have little time to rest. By the end of the rut, most bulls are skinny and have many battle scars. They also shed their antlers at this time. Some bulls are so worn down by the rut that they do not survive the winter.

Throughout the fall, caribou travel toward their wintering grounds. Some lakes freeze so hard they can walk across them, but they must zig-zag around mountains and other barriers. The extra distance adds up. Some caribou may walk up to 3,000 miles (4,828 kilometers) in a year! Most herds reach the taiga before darkness takes over for the winter. Bulls separate into groups called bachelor herds, and cows with calves form their own small groups. All of them begin to paw the snow, digging for lichens.

Finding enough winter food is a challenge to all caribou. Peary caribou, living all year on treeless islands, graze on high ridges where the wind blows away most of the snow. Ice-crusted snow on the tundra forces most other caribou into the forests, where the soft snow is easier to dig. In mid-winter, a caribou may spend 12 hours each day digging 10 to 15 craters, to get enough to eat.

The first autumn snowfall is a sign that caribou must hurry to their wintering grounds.

Caribou compete for the best feeding spots, stealing craters by threatening with their antlers or hooves. Because cows keep their antlers all winter, they can often defend their craters from bigger bulls. Mother caribou do share their feeding holes with their young.

Calves stay with their mothers all winter. They learn where to find food and how to avoid predators. Most important, they get to know the herd's daily movements and how the patterns change with the seasons. A calf's first year is its hardest. About half of them die before their first birthday. Calves that survive often migrate to the calving grounds with their mothers, then separate into groups with other yearlings. Male calves will probably live to be about 10 years old, and females live to about 15 years.

A young caribou, such as this woodland calf, learns to find food
for itself mostly by watching what its mother eats at different times of the year.

Caribou require a large territory to find enough food and raise their young.
They also need a good source of clean water.

What does the future hold for caribou? The barren-ground herds sometimes grow or shrink, and no one knows exactly why. And no one is certain how to solve the problems causing Peary and woodland caribou populations to decline. But scientists understand that too much logging can damage the taiga, roads can scar the tundra, and oil exploration can disturb caribou migration. Cows with young calves are especially sensitive to changes on the land. Even more than other wild animals, caribou depend on vast, open spaces to survive.

If the Arctic wilderness is protected for caribou, they will be able to continue their spring and fall journeys across the frozen north, for generation after generation.

Caribou
FUNFACT:

Canada's 25-cent coin has a picture of a caribou's head on one side. The caribou is also found on postage stamps from New Foundland and Alaska.

Internet Sites

You can find out more interesting information about caribou and lots of other wildlife by visiting these web sites.

http://endangered.fws.gov/kids/index.html	U.S. Fish and Wildlife Service
www.animal.discovery.com	Discovery Channel Online
www.EnchantedLearning.com	Disney Online
www.kidsgowild.com	Wildlife Conservation Society
www.kidsplanet.org	Defenders of Wildlife
www.learner.org/jnorth	Journey North
www.nationalgeographic.com/kids	National Geographic Society
www.nwf.org/kids	National Wildlife Federation
www.tnc.org	The Nature Conservancy
www.worldwildlife.org/fun/kids.cfm	World Wildlife Fund
www.wwfcanada.org/satellite/wwfkids	Canadian World Wildlife Fund

Index

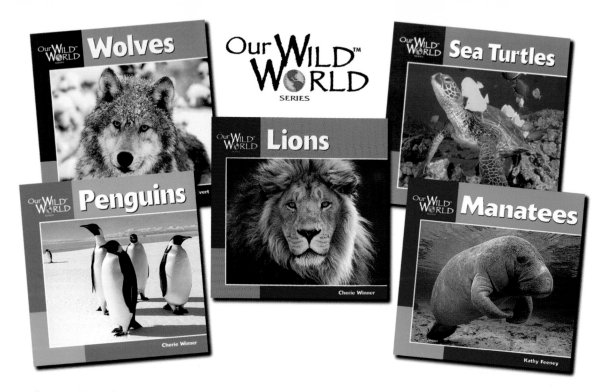

Paperback titles available in the Our Wild World Series:

BISON
ISBN 1-55971-775-0

BLACK BEARS
ISBN 1-55971-742-4

CARIBOU
ISBN 1-55971-812-9

COUGARS
ISBN 1-55971-788-2

DOLPHINS
ISBN 1-55971-776-9

EAGLES
ISBN 1-55971-777-7

LEOPARDS
ISBN 1-55971-796-3

LIONS
ISBN 1-55971-787-4

MANATEES
ISBN 1-55971-778-5

MOOSE
ISBN 1-55971-744-0

PENGUINS
ISBN 1-55971-810-2

POLAR BEARS
ISBN 1-55971-828-5

SEA TURTLES
ISBN 1-55971-746-7

SEALS
ISBN 1-55971-826-9

SHARKS
ISBN 1-55971-779-3

TIGERS
ISBN 1-55971-797-1

WHALES
ISBN 1-55971-780-7

WHITETAIL DEER
ISBN 1-55971-743-2

WOLVES
ISBN 1-55971-748-3

See your nearest bookseller, or order by phone 1-800-328-3895

NORTHWORD PRESS
Chanhassen, Minnesota